I0756106

THIS BOOK BELONGS TO:

THE WONDERFUL WORLD OF SLOTHS

MIMI JONES

Dedicated to all who love sloths.

ISBN 978-1-958985-97-7

www.joeysavestheday.com

Mimi Books™ Publishing

A Mimi Book

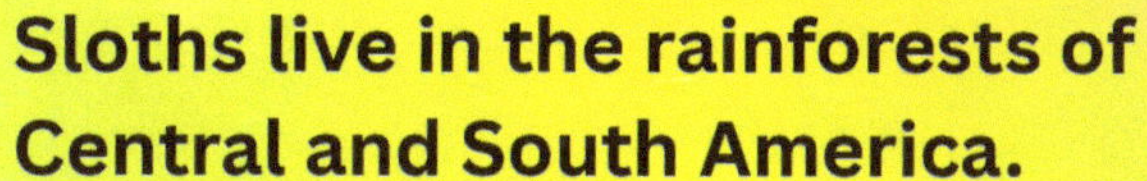

Sloths live in the rainforests of Central and South America.

Central America

South America

Sloths spend almost their entire lives high in the treetops. The canopy keeps them safe from most predators.

CANOPY

The canopy is the top layer of the rainforest, where the branches and leaves of tall trees form a leafy roof high above the ground.

Sloths move slowly to save energy. Their slow pace also helps them avoid being noticed.

SLOW

Sloths are some of the slowest animals on Earth, moving only about 0.24 kilometers per hour. Their slow speed helps them stay hidden from predators.

MAKE THE MOVE

Sloths walk awkwardly on the ground because of their long claws. They move by dragging themselves gently forward.

Sloths have long, curved claws that can grow up to 4 inches. These claws help them hang upside down with almost no effort.
4 INCHES

LEARN

A baby sloth is called a cub. Cubs cling to their mother's belly for months as they learn how to climb.

MIMIC

MEANS TO COPY SOMETHING.

Baby sloths learn everything by watching their moms. They mimic how she climbs, eats, and moves.

8-17

Most sloths weigh between 8 and 17 pounds. That's about as heavy as a small dog.

Sloths can grow up to 2.5 feet long. Their long limbs help them hang easily from branches.

Sloths sleep for 15 to 20 hours a day.
They love resting in cozy tree branches.
ZZZ

Sloths have a very slow metabolism, which means they don't need much food. They eat mostly leaves, buds, and twigs.

DIGEST

A sloth's stomach has multiple compartments to help digest tough leaves. It can take up to a month to fully digest one meal.

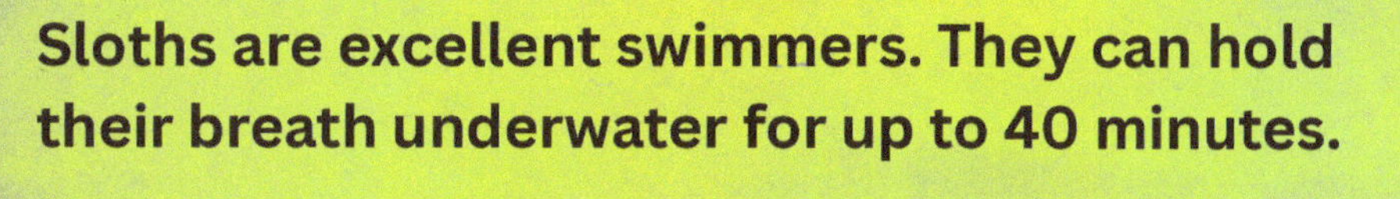

Sloths are excellent swimmers. They can hold their breath underwater for up to 40 minutes.

excellent !

Sloths come in two main types: two-toed and three-toed. Both kinds are gentle and slow-moving.

Two-Toed Sloth
Two claws on front feet
Bigger body
Longer snout

Three-Toed Sloth
Three claws on front feet
Smaller body
Rounder face

Three-toed sloths have a permanent smile on their faces. Their facial structure makes them look happy all the time.

SENSES

Sloths have poor eyesight but excellent senses of smell and touch. These senses help them find food and stay safe.

270 DEGREES

Sloths can turn their heads up to 270 degrees. This helps them look around without moving their bodies.

ALGAE

Algae grows on a sloth's fur and makes it look a little green, helping the sloth blend in with the trees. Sloths even lick the algae for extra nutrients, and tiny insects and moths also live in their fur.

Sloths don't drink much water because they get most of it from leaves. They only drink directly from water sources when needed.

WATER

Sloths can live up to 30 years in the wild. In protected environments, they may live even longer.

30 YEARS

Most sloths are nocturnal, which means they are mainly active at night and rest during the day.

Sloths communicate mostly through soft sounds and body language. Baby sloths make a “bleat” sound to call their mothers.

PREHISTORIC

Sloths have been around for millions of years. Ancient sloths were much larger than today's sloths. Some prehistoric sloths were as big as elephants. These giant ground sloths lived on land instead of in trees.

Sloths are related to anteaters and armadillos. They all belong to a group called Xenarthra.

ANTEATER

ARMADILLO

XENARTHA

OOPOSITE

Sloths' fur grows in the opposite direction of most mammals. It grows from their stomach toward their back to help rainwater run off.

Sloths have a unique way of climbing using a hand-over-hand motion. It looks like they're slowly pulling themselves along.

CALM

Sloths have small, peg-like teeth that never stop growing. They don't have incisors, so they tear leaves with their lips and slowly grind them with their teeth. Sloths are very quiet, calm eaters.

PREFER

Sloths prefer trees like cecropia because the leaves are soft and easy to digest. These trees are like sloth restaurants.

CALMNESS & PATIENCE

Sloths are symbols of calmness and patience. Their slow lifestyle reminds us to take things one step at a time.

Count the sloths.

Thank you for exploring The Wonderful World of Sloths with me. I hope you learned something new and enjoyed meeting these slow, gentle creatures.

If you liked this book, please consider leaving a review. It helps other families discover it too.

See you in the next adventure!

Check out these other interesting books in the Wonderful World of series!

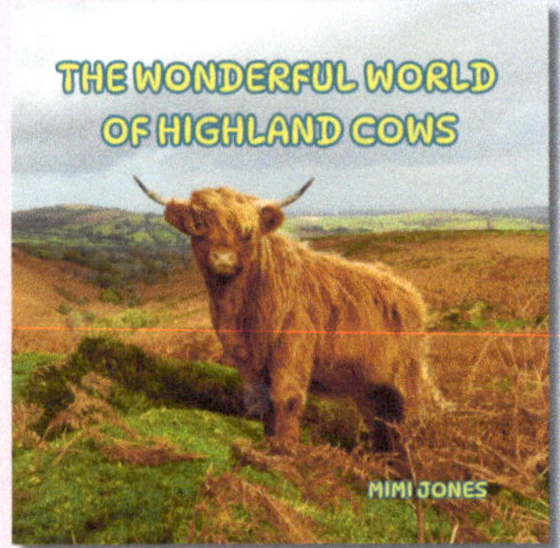

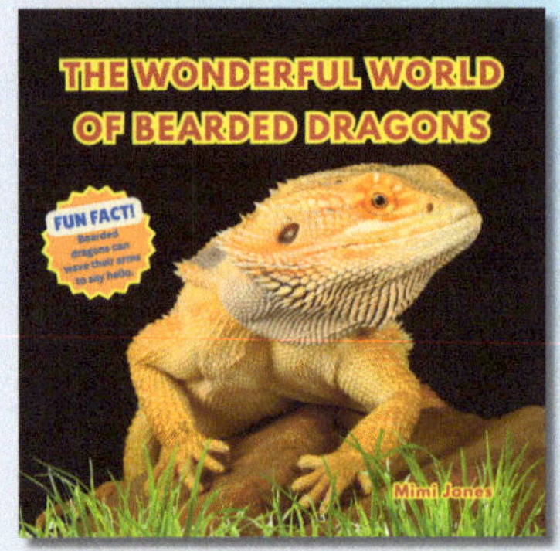

www.mimibooks.com

www.ingramcontent.com/pod-product-compliance
Lightning Source LLC
LaVergne TN
LVHW070158110826
845147LV00002B/439
* 9 7 8 1 9 5 8 9 8 5 9 7 7 *